THE HERITAGE COLLECTION

AWURA ABENA POKUA
Asante Royal and Baule Queen

Letitia deGraft Okyere

Illustrated by Masum Ahmed

Awura Abena Pokua: Asante Royal and Baule Queen
Copyright © 2024 by Letitia deGraft Okyere

Illustrator: Masum Ahmed
Layout designer: Nassim Sarkar

Library of Congress Control Number: 2024900979

All rights reserved.

No part of this publication may be reproduced, stored in a retrieval system, a database, and/or published in any form or by any means, electronic, mechanical, photocopying, recording or otherwise, without the prior written permission of the publisher.

ISBN 978-1-956776-22-5 hardcover
ISBN 978-1-956776-23-2 ebook

Published by Lion's Historian Press
https://www.lionshistorian.net/

In loving memory of

Afia Wirekoa Afrifa

July 6, 1984 – January 31, 2023

A Brief Introduction

Akans are believed to have migrated from the southern portion of the Sahara Desert, now in Mali, to Techiman in present-day Ghana. Over time, differences between the various Akan clans led to separation. Twi-speaking Akans moved from Techiman to areas east of the Comoé River and west of the Afram River. The Oyoko and Oyoko-Adako clans emerged as rulers of Kwaman and Nsuta, respectively, states in south central modern Ghana, some thirty miles apart. These rulers of Kwaman and Nsuta were descendants of Oyoko matriarch Ankyewaa Nyame.

In the mid-1690s, King Osei Tutu I ascended the throne in Kwaman. Ten years later, he organized several Akan states into the Asante Kingdom (or *Asanteman*), assisted by his priest, Okomfo Anokye. Kwaman, renamed Kumasi, became the capital of Asante. To strengthen King Osei Tutu I's position as head of the union of Akan states, Asante lore tells that Okomfo Anokye conjured the Golden Stool (or king's throne) from the heavens. It came down through dark clouds amid thunder, landing on Osei Tutu I's lap and therefore selecting him as the leader of the Asante Kingdom. In Akan tradition, the stool is a king's or chief's symbol of authority. Okomfo Anokye explained that the Golden Stool represented the spirit of this unified Akan group. If the Golden Stool were ever destroyed or captured, it would spell doom for the Asante Kingdom.

Awura Abena Pokua was a niece of King Osei Tutu I, from the Oyoko-Adako royal family of Nsuta. She left Asante when a succession dispute occurred after King Osei Tutu I's death in 1717. She became known by other names, Abraha Pokou and Abla Pokou, when she parted ways with her Asante heritage. Awura Abena Pokua founded a new Akan kingdom, west of Asante.

Contents

Chapter 1:   Arrival of Awura Abena Pokua 1
Chapter 2:   A Happy Childhood 5
Chapter 3:   Grandmother's Training 9
Chapter 4:   Preparation for Marriage 13
Chapter 5:   Birth of Yaw Akoto 17
Chapter 6:   Succession Dispute 21
Chapter 7:   The Walk to Freedom 25
Chapter 8:   Crossing the Comoé River 29
Chapter 9:   Leaving Asante Behind 33
Chapter 10: The Baule Kingdom 35
Epilogue: Baule Akans 39

Appendices
Appendix A: Myths of Awura Abena Pokua 41
Appendix B: Akans of Baule and Asante 42

Glossary 44
Quiz 46
References 47
Fun Fact About Côte d'Ivoire 49
Other Books in the Heritage Collection 50

Chapter - 1

Arrival of Awura Abena Pokua

There is not much known about Awura Abena Pokua's early life. However, she belonged to the Oyoko-Adako royal family of Nsuta in present-day south-central Ghana. It is believed she was born in the mid-1680s before her maternal uncle Osei Tutu I became king of Kwaman. At the time of Abena Pokua's birth, Maanu Kotosii, mother of Osei Tutu I, played a leading role at the Kwaman palace.

There was much rejoicing when Maame Antwiwaa and her warrior husband, Kwadwo Panyin, announced the birth of their daughter, Awura Abena Pokua. She was a beautiful, dark-skinned child with thick, curly, jet-black hair. Elders who visited the royal house to welcome the baby predicted many great deeds in her destiny but then hesitated and toned down their excitement because they also sensed challenges. Maanu Kotosii always hushed up words of Abena Pokua's future trials as she carried her from one elder to another, saying proudly in Twi, "Look at this child, is she not beautiful; she looks just like me." The guests' laughter would chase away menacing clouds hanging over Abena Pokua.

However, the dark prophecy concerning Abena Pokua's future would return. Akan custom demanded a mother introduce her new child to the community. Days after Abena Pokua's birth, Maame Antwiwaa strapped

her daughter to her back and did as tradition required. Maame Antwiwaa received gifts of gold dust (*sika futuro*) and other items as many residents remarked on Abena Pokua's beauty. But again, those elders with insight could not help but mention a troubled future, though each smoothened over the premonitions with good wishes. They encouraged Maame Antwiwaa to do all she could to keep her child from harm.

Chapter - 2

A Happy Childhood

Awura Abena Pokua grew up sheltered by her parents and extended family. She had a happy childhood with her younger sisters, Ama Yeboaa and Afua Nyinsemaa. Even though Abena Pokua and her sisters were from the Oyoko-Adako royal family, they spent time in Kumasi. During the reign of King Osei Tutu I, palace guests often heard the girls' laughter as they played in the gardens. When guests asked King Osei Tutu I about them, he always answered, "Yes, those are my daughters. When I am gone to be with my ancestors, the eldest, called Abena Pokua, will become queen mother of our unified state." In Akan culture, the right of inheritance runs through the mother. Therefore, daughters of Osei Tutu I's sisters, as well as those of his maternal female cousins, were considered his children.

King Osei Tutu I enjoyed asking Abena Pokua to attend his court. He knew that his guests would be charmed by her beauty and poise. Even at such a young age, Abena Pokua gracefully entered her uncle's court after being summoned, acknowledged her uncle the king with a bow, greeted the guests from left to right as custom demands, asked if their journey to the palace was peaceful, and then offered refreshments. A quick glance at the king showed him beaming with pride. Abena Pokua was truly the star of the royal Oyoko-Adako family, destined for great things in the kingdom.

After King Osei Tutu I dismissed Abena Pokua, she ran to the palace residence to change back into her play clothes before joining her sisters. If Maame Antwiwaa did not have any chores for the girls, they stayed out all afternoon. Sometimes, the girls went with servants to fetch water. Abena Pokua was not allowed to swim in the river. One day, she might be queen mother and was not allowed to take part in activities that put her life at risk. Abena Pokua often wondered what playing in the water felt like; she wished she could take a dip with her sisters.

Chapter - 3

Grandmother's Training

Awura Abena Pokua was mature beyond her years. Hence, King Osei Tutu I saw she would benefit from early training in customs and traditions, history, and politics. Abena Pokua began her training with Grandmother Maanu Kotosii before her tenth birthday. The young princess loved Nana, as the king's mother was fondly known, very much, and was excited about spending special time with her. As the senior female at the palace, she represented wisdom and carried knowledge of state and family history. Nana Maanu was keen to share this with Abena Pokua.

At the time, Twi-speaking Akan states were in a period of significant political instability. The demands from Denykira's king had increased. Abena Pokua learned how Grand-uncle King Obiri Yeboa tried to unify several Akan states as a step towards ending their vassal status to the powerful Denykira Kingdom. King Obiri Yeboa died during war with Domaa and Osei Tutu I became king. The new king knew that he must first reform the military before continuing with the late King Obiri Yeboa's expansion plans.

One cool afternoon, during a lesson with Nana, the war horn was sounded. Abena Pokua almost jumped onto Nana's lap from fright. King Osei Tutu I was going to war against the Domaa king with the reformed Kumasi army. He sought revenge for the late King Obiri Yeboa's death. Abena Pokua hugged

Nana before she rushed home to say goodbye to her father, Kwadwo Panyin, a senior warrior in the king's army. Many days passed in Kwaman before news of Domaa's defeat reached the palace. There was a long celebration when King Osei Tutu I and his warriors returned home.

After this victory, King Osei Tutu I merged many independent Akan states into the Amantoo coalition. The Amantoo coalition would later become known as the Asante Kingdom. Abena Pokua understood the changes that had taken place. Why Kwaman had been renamed Kumasi and was the capital of the Amantoo coalition. Why Uncle Osei Tutu I had been selected leader of the coalition. "Aaah," Abena Pokua said, "That is why Uncle is no longer *Kumasihene* but *Amantoohene*." "Yes," Nana replied, adding, "And the Golden Stool, the Amantoohene's throne, holds the spirit of our new nation." Abena Pokua could not wait to share her knowledge with her sisters.

Chapter - 4

Preparation for Marriage

Awura Abena Pokua was heartbroken when Nana Maanu Kotosii died a few years later. After the mourning period, King Osei Tutu I's niece, Nyarko Kusi Amoa, became the first queen mother of the Amantoo coalition of states. Abena Pokua knew that Nyarko Kusi Amoa did not like her very much; she was not going to have any fun in class. As the queen mother, Nyarko Kusi Amoa would be responsible for training the younger females of the royal household. Oh, how Abena Pokua missed Nana.

Just as Abena Pokua feared, Queen Mother Nyarko changed her lessons from history and politics to preparations for marriage. Queen Mother Nyarko told Abena Pokua that she had no chance of becoming queen mother because there were others who were more qualified. Abena Pokua accepted the change, learning how to cook and keep a home. Queen Mother Nyarko instructed palace servants to take Abena Pokua to the farm. With tears rolling down her face, Abena Pokua planted or harvested crops at the farm while her cousins sat in class learning state and court protocol.

When Abena Pokua turned sixteen years, Queen Mother Nyarko informed King Osei Tutu I that it was time for his niece to get married and he agreed. Within a short period, Queen Mother Nyarko identified a suitor for Abena Pokua. Queen Mother Nyarko was keen to get Abena Pokua out of the

palace. Abena Pokua was married to a farmer called Akwasi Mensa, even though King Osei Tutu I could not attend the marriage ceremonies. King Osei Tutu I was in a war against King Ntim Gyakari of Denkyira.

The Amantoo coalition forces needed to break Denkyira's hold over them. Denkyira's tribute required from vassal states had become too burdensome. So, when King Osei Tutu I and his forces defeated Denkyira in 1701, it was a special time in the history of Abena Pokua's state. After Denkyira fell, the Amantoo coalition, with newly expanded borders, became known as the Asante Kingdom (or Asanteman). Amantoohene, King Osei Tutu I, got the title *Asantehene* (king of Asante) and Nyarko Kusi Amoa, *Asantehemaa* (queen mother of Asante). A married Abena Pokua could not join in the celebrations. Her husband, Akwasi Mensa, did not care about her royal status and insisted she was needed at the farm.

Chapter - 5

Birth of Yaw Akoto

Awura Abena Pokua's marriage to Akwasi Mensa was not a happy one. When, after a year of marriage, there was no sign of a child, Akwasi Mensa was cruel, calling her names. Akwasi blamed Abena Pokua, while the royal family thought it was Akwasi's fault. Women in the community laughed at Abena Pokua, shaming her for being childless. Abena Pokua paid them no attention, hopeful her situation would change for the better.

Abena Pokua still had no child after five years and her family ended the marriage. Abena Pokua remarried two years later but remained childless. However, in 1717, after ten years, she gave birth to a son named Yaw Akoto. Abena Pokua and Maame Antwiwaa were full of joy. A few days after his birth, Abena Pokua strapped Yaw Akoto to her back and took him around the town, just as Maame Antwiwaa had done with her.

Abena Pokua went to the wise old woman called Aberewa Ampen, who took a long glance at Yaw Akoto and back at Abena Pokua. Aberewa Ampen reminded Abena Pokua of the old dark prediction, adding that time was getting close. "Awura Abena Pokua, remain determined and courageous, follow your destiny," Aberewa Ampen said. A cold shiver went down Abena Pokua's spine. Leaving Aberewa Ampen's home in a hurry, Abena Pokua headed toward her mother's palace residence.

As Abena Pokua entered the palace grounds, she heard wailing. Walking closer to her mother's apartment, she saw women dressed in black throwing up balls of sand over themselves. Osei Tutu I, founding king of Asante, had been shot during Asante's conflict with the Akyem. To make matters worse, his body had fallen into the Pra River and was washed away. There could not be a proper king's burial.

Chapter - 6

Succession Dispute

Awura Abena Pokua worried about who would be selected to replace Osei Tutu I. Council elders decided on Nana Darko, Abena Pokua's brother. Nana Darko had the necessary qualifications: leadership skills and knowledge of history, politics, and customs and traditions. Abena Pokua approved and indicated her support, along with her mother, sisters, and other members of the Oyoko-Adako royal family.

Abena Pokua sensed trouble when Opoku Ware I returned from the battle with the Akyem. He was displeased by the preparations for Nana Darko's enstoolment (or coronation). Opoku Ware I, Queen Mother Nyarko Kusi Amoa's son, claimed the throne; he argued that Osei Tutu I chose him as his successor before his death. Opoku Ware I's supporters killed Nana Darko while he slept and, later, Maame Antwiwaa. Kwadwo Panyin, Abena Pokua's father, could not help, he had died years earlier.

The family conflict that erupted spread across Asante, causing destruction and death. Tension between the different Akan groups within the union grew, as vassal states conquered by Osei Tutu I saw a chance to overthrow Asante as their master. After three years of bloodshed, Opoku Ware I was made king in 1720. Those who had supported Nana Darko worried about their safety. They began to discuss the option of leaving Asante.

Abena Pokua and many others planned their exit. She took royal regalia including King Obiri Yeboa's stool (or throne) and King Osei Tutu I's golden umbrella and sword. Abena Pokua led the large party from Nsuta, northeast of Kumasi, when King Opoku Ware I was on a military campaign. The migrants included the Warebo and three other groups of nobility.

Abena Pokua took the group westwards, hoping thick forests would provide protection as they trekked for a place to settle. When King Opoku Ware I heard about the departure, he sent Asante warriors to find and return them to the kingdom. He did not want a separate clan of nobility threatening his reign. Abena Pokua heard of the king's search party and realized they would be killed if found. She had to ensure they avoided capture at all costs.

Chapter - 7

The Walk to Freedom

Awura Abena Pokua led her group past towns and villages in Asante. The journey was difficult. Many chiefs had sworn allegiance to King Opoku Ware I, and thus, it was unsafe to take breaks in these communities. Abena Pokua established a leadership council, and it assigned roles. Scouts were sent ahead, returning at intervals with information on whether it was safe to travel in the direction headed. Hunters searched for game. Each day's supply was distributed to families for meals based on need. At sunset, they all settled by a body of water for the night before moving forward in the morning.

The migrants went to their ancestral home of Tanoso, on the Tano River. Abena Pokua's sister, Afua Nyinsemaa stayed behind to pray for the migrants' safety. The group went south to Sefwi, then southwest to Aowin. They blended in as much as possible with these western states to make it difficult for Opoku Ware I's warriors to track them. They cooked western foods and dressed like westerners. The Sefwi and Aowin welcomed the visitors because they resented having Asante as overlord. These western states had been conquered by King Osei Tutu I a few years before his death.

Abena Pokua, now the matriarch of a new runaway nation, changed her name to Abenlema Poku and adopted the Western accent, making a

final break from her past life as an Asante royal. Over time, it is believed Abenlema was reduced to Abla. One evening, scouts reported that Asante warriors had discovered their hiding place and were headed towards them. King Opoku Ware I's men had instructions to kill all those who refused to return to Kumasi. Abena Pokua and her group quickly packed up and moved further west, unsure where the path taken would lead them.

Chapter - 8

Crossing the Comoé River

Awura Abena Pokua and her migrant group walked day and night until arriving at the shores of the Comoé River. They would be safe from the pursuing Asante warriors after crossing the river. What a relief! The priest insisted on a sacrifice to the river to secure final freedom. So, the women gathered earrings, bracelets, and amulets, but the priest rejected the items, shouting that the river demanded something of greater value than gold knick-knacks. Abena Pokua, with a sinking feeling in her stomach, asked the priest what was considered valuable enough for the river. "A mother must offer her young child," he answered.

A quick glance at the women told Abena Pokua that none of the mothers was willing to sacrifice her child. She had only one option left. As if in a trance, Abena Pokua unwrapped her precious and only child, Yaw Akoto, from her back and waded into the river. With both arms outstretched, she raised Yaw Akoto above her head and threw him into the river. As she watched the river take her son away, her legs gave way, and she began to sink. Before she fell, three women rushed to her aid, pulling her ashore.

Council elders then gave the call for everyone to march through the river, led by the tallest men in the group. Abena Pokua, assisted by three women, were the last to cross. She was in shock and not responding to conversations

around her. Soon after Abena Pokua and the women reached the shore on the other side, heavy rains came down, flooding the riverbanks. They looked back and saw Opoku Ware I's soldiers, angry that Abena Pokua and the group had escaped for good.

Chapter - 9

Leaving Asante Behind

Awura Abena Pokua collapsed into the wet soil after crossing. She remembered Aberewa Ampen's words, warning of future pain and challenges. Abena Pokua wailed for her son, throwing her arms up into the air, screaming, "*Ba no awu*" (the child is dead) repeatedly. Abena Pokua could not be comforted, large tears falling from her eyes. She became weak because of her sadness. The group stayed by the Comoé River until she regained strength to lead them to a new home.

After many days, the migrants prepared to leave the banks of the Comoé. A clan of warriors sought permission from Abena Pokua to stay behind. If there were any threats from Asante, it would reach them first. As warriors, they were better placed to repel any efforts to capture the migrants. This sub-group took Osei Tutu I's golden umbrella and sword as their symbol of unity. Items that were part of the royal regalia removed by Abena Pokua as she planned to leave Asante.

Other sub-sections settled along the way, including the torch bearers and foot soldiers, creating more Akan groups in the region. Abena Pokua guided the remaining migrants toward the Bandama River, now in Côte d'Ivoire. The struggle was not over, though; they would have to fight those already settled in the area for a new home.

Chapter - 10

The Baule Kingdom

Awura Abena Pokua's search for fertile land took the migrants southbound to the Tiassalé region. Though they faced some resistance, the travelers subdued local inhabitants. After a while, Abena Pokua journeyed further north, leaving behind a group of migrants. She founded Tano Sakassou, west of Bouaké, as her capital town. The group made Abena Pokua queen and adopted the name "Baule," said to be corrupted from ba no awu, in recognition of her sacrifice of Yaw Akoto for the new Akan nation. Also, Baule was the historical name of an area in that region.

Existing residents of towns and villages around Bouaké resented the presence of the new arrivals. The Senufo people from the north attacked the new settlers. Abena Pokua and her warriors defeated them. The migrants were attacked by the Guru people from the west; again, Abena Pokua battled the Guru, who withdrew in defeat.

Abena Pokua would have to crush an old enemy before finding peace. After the defeat of the Denkyira by King Osei Tutu I, some Denkyira people settled close to Bouaké with King Ntim Gyakari's stool. When they heard that an Asante royal was establishing a new kingdom nearby, they attacked in revenge for Ntim Gyakari's death. Abena Pokua and her warriors defeated them, seizing the throne.

By 1730, Abena Pokua had either conquered or won over all her enemies, and the new Baule Kingdom began to grow. Abena Pokua established the Baule Adako clan, unified with the stools of Obiri Yeboa (which she took when leaving Asante) and Ntim Gyakari of Denkyira (a war trophy). Back in Asante, the Great Oath of Silence, known as *Ntam Kesea*, was taken. This ensured that the killing of Nana Darko and separation of Abena Pokua and the migrants were not spoken of.

Abena Pokua reigned for thirty years, and after her death, she was buried near her capital city. Abena Pokua was succeeded by her niece, Akwa Boni. The right to rule the migrant people remained with the Warebo who claimed Abena Pokua as a direct ancestress. Visitors to Abidjan, the largest city in République de Côte d'Ivoire, will find a metal statue of Abena Pokua at the République Square, referred to as Reine Pokou (Queen Pokou).

Epilogue

Baule Akans

Decades after Awura Abena Pokua's death in the 1760s, the Baule Kingdom grew to encompass a large portion of land between the Bandama and Comoé rivers, including Bouaké and Yamoussoukro in southeast République de Côte d'Ivoire. The Baule became a formidable state and acquired wealth as the land was full of natural resources, including gold. The Baule Kingdom became the center of the cocoa industry, and leading supplier of rubber and coffee. In the 1880s, the Baule were colonized by the French after a long battle where the nation was defeated. Since full independence from the French in 1960, the Baule have produced two presidents, Félix Houphouët-Boigny and Henri Konan Bédié. The Baule are known for their unique wooden statues and clay pottery.

As time passed, the rift between the Baule and Asante healed. Regalia taken by Abena Pokua were returned to Asante. In 1894, during the official enstoolment of King Prempeh I, a large Baule entourage led by Nana Kouamé Guie attended the event in Kumasi. The link between the Baule and Asante has continued to develop. President Henri Konan Bédié visited Manhyia Palace (home of the Asante King) twice and Nsuta, his ancestral home once. When former President Bédié died, Baule representatives traveled to Kumasi to inform King Osei Tutu II in 2024.

Appendix A

Myths of Awura Abena Pokua

There are two primary myths describing how Awura Abena Pokua and her group crossed the Comoé River to safety. With one lore, after Abena Pokua threw her son into the river and he was "swallowed up" by the waves, the earth began to tremble violently. A herd of hippopotami came to the river's surface, forming a bridge. The migrant group walked on the backs of the hippopotami to the other side. After the last person crossed, the hippopotami disappeared.

The other fable also describes an intense earthquake, this time uprooting a large silk-cotton tree on the edge of the river. The tree fell across the river, creating a bridge. When the last person crossed, another earthquake broke the tree into pieces, and the river washed it away.

In both versions, Asante warriors on the banks of the Comoé River had no way of crossing because the river level was high and dangerous. However, many experts point out that the Comoé River was low and easy to cross because of rocks visible on the surface. Then there are those who doubt the sacrifice of a child, arguing that gifts of personal value were more likely to have been tossed into the river.

Appendix B

Akans of Baule and Asante

When Awura Abena Pokua and her group left Asante, they kept some old Akan/Asante customs. They continued to name children after the day of the week on which they were born. These are called *kradin* or soul names. However, to show a separation from Asante, they modified the order. Thus, Baule soul names do not exactly match Akan or Asante soul names, although the similarity is easy to see.

For example, the names for children born on Saturday in Akan/Baule are *Koffi* (male) and *Affoué* (female). But for Akan/Twi, spoken by the Asante, a male child born on Friday is *Kofi*, and a female, *Afua*. In Akan/Baule, boys born on Sunday are *Kouamé* and girls, *Amoin*. In Akan/Twi, Saturday-born boys are *Kwame* and girls, *Ama*.

Weekday	Baule		
	Day Name	Male	Female
Sunday	Monnie	Kouamé	Amoin
Monday	Kissie	Kouassi	Akissi
Tuesday	Djole	Kouadjo	Adjoua
Wednesday	Mlan	Konan	Amlan
Thursday	Ouwe	Kouakou	Ahou
Friday	Yah	Yao	Aya
Saturday	Foue	Koffi	Affoué

Weekday	Asante Twi		
	Day Name	Male	Female
Sunday	Kwasiada	Kwasi	Akosua
Monday	Ɛdwoada	Kwadwo	Adwoa
Tuesday	Ɛbenada	Kwabena	Abena
Wednesday	Wukuada	Kwaku	Akua
Thursday	Yawoada	Yaw	Yaa
Friday	Efiada	Kofi	Afua
Saturday	Memeneda	Kwame	Ama

The Akan of present-day Ghana have names for children based on the order of birth by one woman. Baule Akans in Côte d'Ivoire kept this custom with similar-sounding names. For example, the third child by one mother is called *I'nsan* (for both boys and girls) in Baule Akan. In Asante Twi and other Akan groups in Ghana, it is *Mensah* (for boys) and *Mansa* (for girls).

Birth Order	Baule	Akan
Third child	I'nsan	Mensah/Mansa
Ninth child	N'Goran	Akron/Nkroma/Nkrumah
Tenth child	Brou	Badu/Baduwaa
Eleventh child	Loukou	Duku
Twelfth child	N'Gbin	Dunu

Glossary

Oyoko	This is an Akan clan. In Akan culture, a clan (or *abusua*) refers to a group of people with the same maternal ancestor. The Oyoko-Adako clan split from the Oyoko.
Amantoo	The Akan coalition formed during the reign of King Osei Tutu I. After defeating Denkyira, the Amantoo coalition became known as the Kingdom of Asante.
Denkyira	An Akan kingdom founded in the 1500s by the Agona clan in the southwestern area of modern-day Ghana. It was the overlord of many Akan states in the region until its defeat by King Osei Tutu I and the Amantoo coalition forces.
Queen mother	An important female traditional ruler. A queen mother rules alongside kings and chiefs. She presides over a court where she dispenses justice and leads panels that select kings and chiefs when there is a vacancy.
Enstoolment	In the Akan tradition, when kings or chiefs are appointed, the ceremony is known as enstoolment, like being enthroned. The Akan king sits on a stool, regarded as his throne or the symbol of his authority.
Premonition	A strong feeling or sense that something either positive or negative is going to happen.
Hene	A suffix meaning king or chief depending on the state to which it refers. The Asantehene is the king of Asante.

Tano River	This river flows from Techiman in present-day Ghana and enters the Atlantic Ocean through Côte d'Ivoire. Its length is estimated at 250 miles.
Comoé River	This river is about 470 miles long and begins in Burkina Faso, flowing through Côte d'Ivoire and emptying into the Gulf of Guinea.
Bandama River	This is the longest river in Côte d'Ivoire, with a length of 500 miles. It flows through the artificial Lake Kossou, created as part of the Kossou Dam.
King Ntim Gyakari	The king of Denkyira conquered by King Osei Tutu I and the Amantoo coalition forces.
Baule	Akans living between the Comoé and Bandama rivers in Côte d'Ivoire. They were led to the area by their ancestress, Awura Abena Pokua of the Asante Oyoko-Adako royal family. Predominant sources put the timing of the migration after the death of King Osei Tutu I.
Sika futuro	Gold dust, used as currency or money. When Osei Tutu I became king, it became more widely used.

Quiz

1. Where was Awura Abena Pokua born?

    (a) Baule
    (b) Asante
    (c) Ivory Coast
    (d) Bandama

2. What was the name of the Akan coalition before it became known as the Kingdom of Asante?

    (a) Amantoo
    (b) Nsuta
    (c) Kumasi
    (d) Baule

3. Who forced Awura Abena Pokua into early marriage?

    (a) Nana Maanu Kotosii
    (b) King Osei Tutu I
    (c) Maame Antwiwaa
    (d) Nyarko Kusi Amoa

4. What new kingdom did Awura Abena Pokua rule after she left Asante?

    (a) Nsuta
    (b) Warebo
    (c) Baule
    (d) Kumasi

Quiz Answers: BADC

References

Adou, Kouamé. "Memory and Exile: The Transatlantic and Diasporic Dimensions of the Myth of Ashanti Princess Abla Pokou." *Études Littéraires Africaines*, no. 139, 2015, pp. 145-159.

Gedzi, Victor S. "The Asante of Ghana." *International Journal of African Society Cultures and Traditions*, vol. 2, no. 3, 2014, pp. 20-26.

Tadjo, Véronique. *Queen Pokou: Concerto for a Sacrifice*. Translated from French by Amy Baram Reid, Ayebia Clarke Publishing Limited, 2009.

McCaskie, T.C. "Denkyira in the Making of Asante, 1660-1720." *Journal of African History*, vol. 48, 2007, pp. 1-25.

Weiskel, Timothy C. "The Precolonial Baule: A Reconstruction." *Cahiers d'Études Africaines*, vol. 18, no. 72, 1978, pp. 503-560.

Davidson, Basil. *A History of West Africa 1000-1800*. Longman, 1977.

Fynn, John K. "Opoku Ware." *Encyclopedia Africana Dictionary of African Biography*, Volume 1, Ethiopia – Ghana, edited by L.H. Ofosu-Appiah, Reference Publications Inc., 1977, pp. 288-289.

Fynn, John K. "Osei Tutu." *Encyclopedia Africana Dictionary of African Biography*, Volume 1, Ethiopia – Ghana, edited by L.H. Ofosu-Appiah, Reference Publications Inc., 1977, pp. 294-295.

Adu Boahen, A. "When Did Osei Tutu Die?" *Transactions of the Historical Society of Ghana*, vol. 16, no. 1, June 1975, pp. 87-92.

Fun Fact About the République de Côte d'Ivoire

The world's largest church is in Yamoussoukro, the administrative capital of Côte d'Ivoire. The Basilica of Our Lady of Peace was built over four years, from 1985-1989. It has stained-glass windows and white columns with a huge pearl dome. During the many years of conflict in the country, citizens sought refuge at the church because they knew that soldiers would never attack it.

Other Books in the Heritage Collection

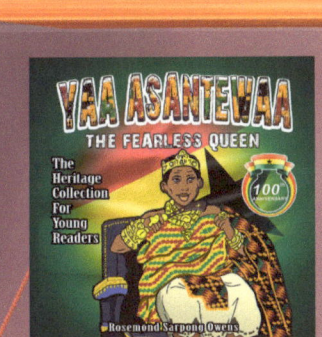
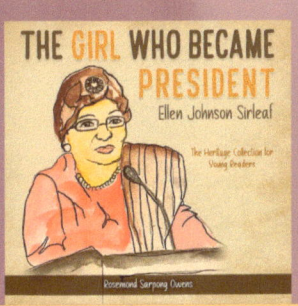
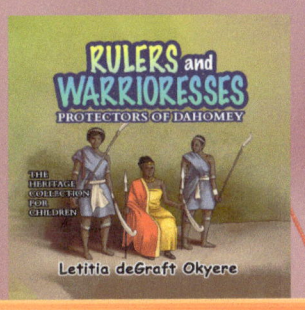

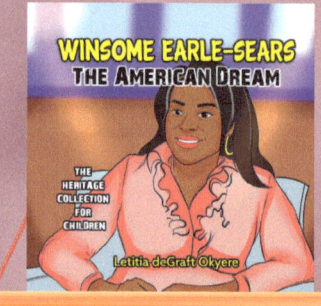
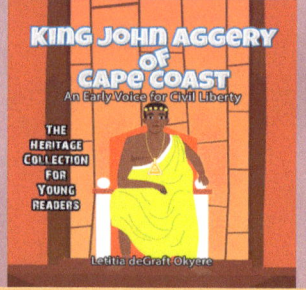

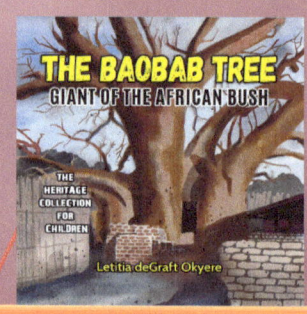
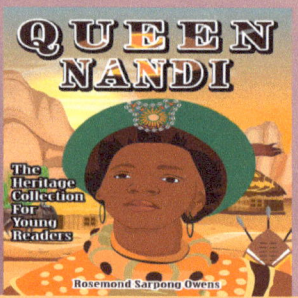

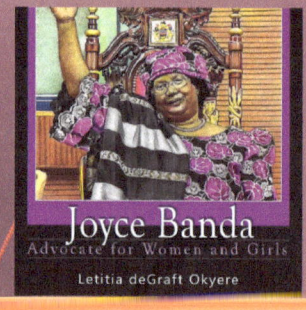

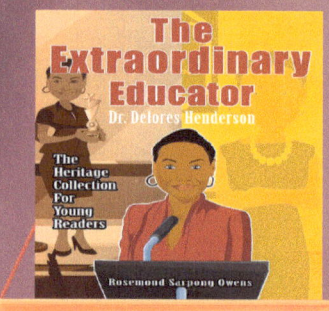
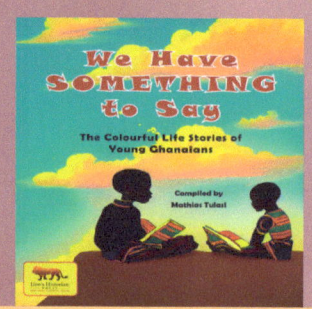
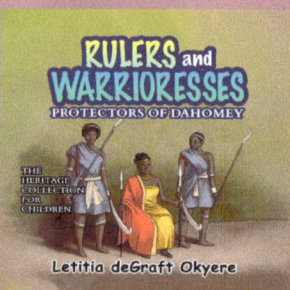